Elsewhere

Jack Little
Elsewhere

20/20 **EYEWEAR**
PAMPHLET SERIES
2015

First published in 2015 by Eyewear Publishing Ltd
74 Leith Mansions, Grantully Road
London W9 1LJ United Kingdom

Typeset with graphic design by Edwin Smet
Printed in England by Lightning Source
All rights reserved © 2015 *Jack Little*

The right of Jack Little to be identified as author of this work has been asserted in accordance with section 77 of the Copyright, Designs and Patents Act 1988

ISBN 978-1-908998-70-5
WWW.EYEWEARPUBLISHING.COM

Thank you
to Karenina for her love and inspiration. The Little and Osnaya families. My friends whom I have met through The Ofi Press. Miss Teasdale. Andrew McMillan for his support. A big thank you to Todd Swift at Eyewear. To Luis Cotto-Vasallo and my friends at The American Legion, and to all of the people of Mexico City who make life so exciting and fulfilling no matter how far away I am from home.

Al-hamdu lillahi rabbil 'alamin.

*Los únicos paraísos no vedados
a los hombres, son los paraísos
perdidos.*

Jorge Luis Borges

for Karenina

Table of contents

9   *Elsewhere*
10 *Songs of Xochimilco*
11 *Favourite Time of Day*
12 *Night Sky*
13 *City Sleeping*
14 *Üllői Út*
15 *Russian Doll Falling*
16 *The Cymbalist's Moment*
18 *A Lament for Ponciano Díaz*
19 *'6 Toros 6'*
20 *The Last Train to London*
21 *Robin Grown Old*
22 *Remembering an Old Friend*
23 *An Old Synthonia Lullaby*
24 *Wasp*
25 *Widow's Gift*
26 *Medicine Woman*
27 *Photo of My Mother's Mother*
28 *Coffee Stains*
29 *Swimming Lessons*

Elsewhere

Searching his pockets
he left and learnt new languages
in a city with a name he could
not pronounce

and his house was built upon the crooked roof
of an old scrap dealer's yard, the 'tick, crash, bang'
of workers smashing last century's washing machines
clashed with a sun god he did not know:

he drank with them but couldn't
understand the roaring new words
that bounced like motorbikes on summer roads

but learnt how to smile
and buy beer for all

and when purple night sank her boats
and the lights went out with rain,
he withdrew himself from the magic of elsewhere
and rejoined the boys of home –
the language of his father crisp and warm,

but of another time.

Songs of Xochimilco

Your boats have names like 'Lupita' and 'Ana María',
bright splashes of margarita on a flower girl's dress, you sing.

The canals of Xochimilco once carried maize and drumbeats to market
and Aztec Gods blessed mythical flowers with water as cempazuchitl
and bougainvilleas flourished on earthy floating gardens.

Now gondolas of drunks in mutinous festivity rule
where gaudy mariachis sing old songs of lost loves
and kayaks pass by close to your finger tips:
the sweet smell of chili and icy beer are medicines
against the sticky sun that you lick from your lips.

Beneath your oars, the axolotl navigates olive inky waters:
forever young and ancient, a deity of lightning and death
grown naïve to man's fleeting upper hand.

The end is coming. Our few pesos last only for an hour and Tenochtitlan
has long since gone. Man cannot demand from nature forever when
urban sprawl gnaws at her fertile land. Canals of Xochimilco,
soon your music shall be lost to us. We, the unlistening keepers of paradise.

Favourite Time of Day

A wall, translucent yellow
pink to gold and back to pale
the calming shadow of evening

The last sun tastes of fried egg
       – I lick her from my lips –
from the terracotta red
brick, slick daylight slides
over the horizon

and all around is darkness

Night Sky
> *for Don Cellini*

Beyond my window, the sky swirls night black
shadows, I trace my reflection in the windowpane
before turning hastily to bed. Puzzle pieces, dream
formations, images of the moon at different latitudes:

> Caracas, Buenos Aires, Montevideo,
> Panamá and São Paulo

my mind awaits them all, the visits of feather capped
gods of heavy ancientness, the smell of other
worlds that cling to my bedclothes: the heat of night
and journeys to far away temples of unknown sun people…

> I await Bogotá
> I await Lima,
> Barranquilla, Brasília, Managua, Bucaramanga…

Asunción… and on and on – all memories learnt
from news stories, a crack of light breaking the sky
and reminding me of the classroom globes of childhood.

City Sleeping

Heaving sun slip away unnoticed, the
crowded streets aswash with the crock
of yesterday's gossip dripping
from her tongue: she sleeps.

But restless, the bustle does not cease
but deadens; rusty beetles crawl
back to their nests,
hives buzzing rhythmically

to a dreamland, of filth contaminated air
painting pictures, dancing in the sky
your colours purple – your body
fat to bursting with the business of the day.

Üllői Út
>   *for Árpád and Eva*

In Budapest,
I breathe in fairy dust,
the white, the light sub-zero
liquor of winter sunrise.

Rub hands, sweat under seven layers
smell kifli bread and coffee steam – the tram ride
shudders from Albertfalva, crosses the Danube
the huddle of islands, palaces stand guard,

I *umm* and *ahh* at strange vowels on street signs
>   gravelly, short and stout like pork pie.

Russian Doll Falling

A Russian doll is an easy metaphor,
        in its death dance
spinning on cold wooden edges
        'til tipping point

Until you break, until you crack in twos, fours...
        smooth and lipstick red, matryoshka doll:
coffee cool wooden carvings on the inside
        a chrysalis, a surprise of resting air.

The Cymbalist's Moment

Lizard basking in the sun, cascading
hours of practice

The eruption of wait… wait… wait…
from grandiose, octopus arms – a tantric crescendo,
your eyes shine like poetry, your body
wobbles with pleasure.

The crash of cymbals

And then the reprieve
you're dozing, draped as a curtain
yet to be hung, postcoital walrus
waiting for the sun…

The movement comes to life again
the fiddlers make foreplay with cello-night
playtime: stroke and pluck, but I know you
have your favourites, Gabriela on the drum

you're watching her, sunshine rising
kid grin smiling, undressing each

precise 'POM' – 'POM' – 'POM' beat
with sprawling hands that know exactly what to do

to the moment.

We build again… and again… and again…
and the waves of low tide crash lightly
this time and you won't crash explode, shackled
by the music sheets, but don't worry, I'll
be back next week to watch, waiting

guiltily for your moment.

A Lament for Ponciano Díaz
    after Federico García Lorca

In the *ganadería de Ateneco*
Ponciano Díaz's father fought bulls
with a cloth in one hand and his child in the other.

In the evenings, his brother would sit on the other side of the room
the semi-darkness of the setting sun would leave half shadows:
the day's sandy footprints, the dry spittle at the side of the old man's mouth.

Tonight proclaims his fate is preordained
under the breath of a thousand secret voices:
some of us dwell in our passions more than others.

But before the stains of crimsons spines, and viscera between his sequins
the sunrise will be another part-renewal, grown boastful with swollen pride

    the fight is in his veins.

'6 Toros 6'

At the Plaza de Toros,   Mexico City
colourful posters proclaim   '6 Toros 6'
three matadors kill six bulls   in quick succession

and I am to be in row M   hiding in shadow
far enough away for blood   not to stain my clothes
to be a memory I do not want   I crave new experiences

the bull's broken tooth   conquers my private self
strips shallow layers: the conquest of the man I was
de tres heroes   *de tres muertos*

The Last Train to London

A black tea stewed too long
on Newcastle Central Station platform
waiting for the last train to London.

Cold night breath rises and falls in waves:
a relief like symmetry in the station arches
as a lone man reads the newspaper
over spectacles balanced on the edge of his nose.

An analogue clock clicks hard-edged sounds,
our shared seconds until departure. The absolute
dominates this space between him and I.

I am an extra in the movie of his life, a biopic of one
of the greats, and I play 'man on platform'.

I count grey floor tiles to make up seconds
until the final scene when the fat full moon
will reflect from the gentleman's lenses
and he will glance at me before checking his watch

and I will be validated.

Robin Grown Old

I spent the afternoon in envy of Batman's walking stick
from the shade of the bat cave.

Lost in side-kick alley, I missed the "crash, bang, wallop"
of heroes' hour on Radio 4 as *he* took all the plaudits

babes and girls. And here I am grown old, a shadow
of the 'boy wonder', an object of folly behind the lies
he whispered to me night after night.

And as I watched him dance around his walking stick, I wondered
if he will ever look at me again that way he did that night

when we switched places in the Batmobile, only just for a moment.

Remembering an Old Friend

Many Sunday mornings passed by running
to keep up with pooh sticks, dogs and dad
by the snow drop river side of Henry King's Castle.

Treading carefully from delicate season daffodils
I wish for ice-cream in the North East cold winter wind
and rolling down the castle banks of Henry King's last defence.
For now there is no spring and the great castle of the old hero
Henry King casts a long shadow from Warkworth to
rough edged Mexico, your grey walls

unreal against the spice and bright sun of an impossible
time of year. Sir, my Henry King,

you, the keeper of weekends from a different world,
the keeper of puzzle pieces long since lost.

An Old Synthonia Lullaby

Our baby sleeps softly in the back
crossing the pass at Tees Valley.

Rain pelts the windscreen, the silver
glint of the transporter bridge trickles
between gaps in windscreen wipers.

Mother said Synthonia was an orchestra
for lullabies, the truth an amalgamation
of synthetic ammonia, more magic

than the dreams of our bairn, still unaware
of the chaotic beauty of factory funnels
and the chill of cold air,

        just beyond his touch.

Wasp
    for Theo

Golden Zebra, you told me, children
a galloping horde that made us gasp
– the nest above the pantry,

the hum we never dominated – our hands,
cupped to our eyes, we took turns to look.

Those moments as honeysuckle bloomed
brothers played with wasps, wings
a brilliant black, stripes of lemon slice

from this window here, not stung,
they lead me back to you.

Widow's Gift

A thimbleful of medicine
sits upon the table top. Its reflection
from the mirror, its tiny shadow cast
on yesterday's and all days' dust.

Between my fingertips 'Devon', upside-down,
old souvenir from a place I had never known like you.
The vessel's contents – sand, a crisp yellow liquor;
inside, the smell of vinegar.

A dull ache creeps across my shoulders, slow eyes in semi-darkness,
a tingle. I cup it back, like a baby's hand. A moment passes.
I lie awkwardly on bedclothes that no longer smell of you
observing myths and memories in the ceiling cracks

      much like the nights we slept under the stars.

Medicine Woman
    for Carlotta

The beach at night was empty
but for scavengers and sleeping
hammock-sellers

your husband waited at the house,
his feet in casts: old bull,
never able to write your definition
no matter how he bared his horns

you of the scratching voice,
kind and strange, full as my cup of night time
chocolate ground down smooth,
are sleeping now:

no unnecessary goodbye,
only this memory of our swimming
in the grace of the full moon

Medicine Woman, Mother, Friend,
we lost you to the wind.
I hope to find you one day again,
perhaps on another island.

Photo of My Mother's Mother
   for Pippa and Jane

Image cropped: a half mirror of my mother,
aunts and cousins ten years lost, the eyes
of familiar childhood expressions.

> [Her pristine collar is wrinkled only by a half-century, boxed away.
> The shoulder of another ancient invades the surrounding space.]

I cover her face to explore her forehead, then with two hands
reveal only her eyes. One cheek. I see myself in her chin.

Her smile is an invitation – we talk of lost loved ones,
of brothers, uncles, but there is no sadness or regret

we all just want to be heard; remember those of whom we might have smiled,
be embraced by those still so close but just beyond our finger tips.

Coffee Stains

Memories of goodbyes read like old newspapers,
black, white and wrinkled at the edges –   bad jokes
with coffee stain rings – crop circles – mislaid under
the accumulated years of junk in old wooden boxes

n-w α barely dĺstinguiShaβle heʌdlïne

Yet details remain, the smell of damp and the woodlouse crawling
separate from the whole, the now atomized story of life and old friends
who plug leaking walls with my embellishments:
the ink will run as stories of yesterday's news
quickly become obsolete – fragments, flotsam

torn yet coMfor'tiɳg

Swimming Lessons

Hard as stone, Mexico City
I measure you in cruise liners
far from the sea and hands wider
than the whole of Northumberland

grasping at clanking locks, the cats
in black bin bags are lost in their own
little world – warm and burly the night
light sea, I swear they dance

and what if the rooftop was not to keep
rain out? But to be bathed on, sun bathed
washed in light, watch the ants float by
I swear this is an ocean and I am learning to swim

Acknowledgements

I would like to acknowledge and thank the editors of the following journals and anthologies where versions of some of these poems first appeared: *3:AM Magazine, Myths of the Near Future, The Barehands Anthology, Morphrog, Wasafiri, Under the Radar, The Screech Owl, The Industrial Landscapes Anthology, The Lampeter Review* and *The Curious Symmetry Anthology.*

Notes on the poems;

'Songs of Xochimilco'
Cempazuchitl: Nahuatl for marigold. Also known as 'the flower of the dead'.
Axolotl: A Mexican species of salamander indigenous to Xochimilco.
Tenochtitlan: The ancient capital of the Aztec empire. Today its ruins are located beneath central Mexico City.

'A Lament for Ponciano Díaz'
I first read about the story of Ponciano Díaz in *Brave Blood* by Richard Finks Whitaker, an authoritative book on the history and culture of bull fighting in Mexico.

'Remembering an Old Friend'
This castle in Warkworth, Northumberland was built by King Henry II and appears as a back drop in several scenes to Shakespeare's *Henry IV* part 1.

EYEWEAR PUBLISHING

EYEWEAR 20/20 PAMPHLET SERIES

BEN STAINTON EDIBLES
MEL PRYOR DRAWN ON WATER
MICHAEL BROWN UNDERSONG
MATT HOWARD THE ORGAN BOX
RACHAEL M NICHOLAS SOMEWHERE NEAR IN THE DARK
BETH TICHBORNE HUNGRY FOR AIR
GALE BURNS OPAL EYE
PIOTR FLORCZYK BAREFOOT
LEILANIE STEWART A MODEL ARCHAEOLOGIST
SHELLEY ROCHE-JACQUES RIPENING DARK
SAMANTHA JACKSON SMALL CRIES
V.A. SOLA SMITH ALMOST KID
GEORGE SZIRTES NOTES ON THE INNER CITY
JACK LITTLE ELSEWHERE
DAMILOLA ODELOLA LOST & FOUND
KEITH JARRETT I SPEAK HOME

Lightning Source UK Ltd.
Milton Keynes UK
UKOW06f1157190715

255382UK00008B/84/P